The
ART *of*
NOTICING

ELLEN J. LANGER

For further information, please visit: www.ellenlanger.com and www.langermindfulnessinstitute.com

FOREWORD

This book is the culmination of research on mindlessness and mindfulness conducted from the early 1970's to the present. Many of our studies make clear to me that mindlessness is pervasive. Most of the time we are simply on automatic pilot and are not there to realize we are not there. The research also makes clear that it is possible, indeed reasonably easy, to become more mindful. When we become more mindful, we become happier, healthier, and more effective. It is literally and figuratively enlivening. Mindfulness leaves its imprint on the projects we create. Each of the one-liners in this book has been derived from research conducted over the past 35 years and paired together with paintings created over the past 17 years. Thinking about what each one means should itself promote mindfulness and encourage a more artful life.

Ellen Langer

Facts are just other people's views

CIVIL WAR , acrylic on canvas, 22" x 28"

Where we are is where we've never been

It's hard to go forward when looking back

BACK AND FORTH, acrylic on canvas, 18" x 24"

Expecting change brings stability

HAVE-A-BITE BAR, acrylic on canvas, 48" x 60"

We can find it irritating or see its charm

SUSPENDERS, acrylic on canvas, 8" x 10"

Life would be dull if it all made sense

Being a free spirit is worth the cost

OVER EASY, acrylic canvas, 36" x 48"

Find, don't lose yourself in the activity

EASY RIDER, acrylic on canvas, 36" x 48"

AND not OR

PUPPY LOVE, acrylic on canvas, 24" x 36"

Expecting change brings stability

DOING DISHES, acrylic on canvas, 30" x 40"

Expect to grow

ROOM TO GROW, acrylic on canvas, 32" x 24"

If we take ourselves too seriously,
no one else will

Is it a tragedy or an inconvenience?

HABIT , watercolor, 24" x 48"

Distracted or otherwise attracted?

OTHERWISE ATTRACTED, acrylic on canvas, 10" x 12"

Ask a better question to get a better answer

SCHOOL DAZE, acrylic on canvas, 30" x 40"

Find the novel in the familiar

How we feel is a matter of choice

THREE NANCYS, acrylic on canvas, 22" x 28"

Predict today and lose tomorrow

Mistakes are cues to be in the present

WINDOWS , acrylic on canvas, 36" x 48"

Understanding is better than forgiving

Envy leaves when learning arrives

SUNDAY BRUNCH, acrylic on canvas, 24" x 48"

Be positively negative, say no with a smile

If we don't take the compliment,
we're not vulnerable to the insult

INEBRIATED, acrylic on canvas, 12" x 16"

A centered self is not self-centered

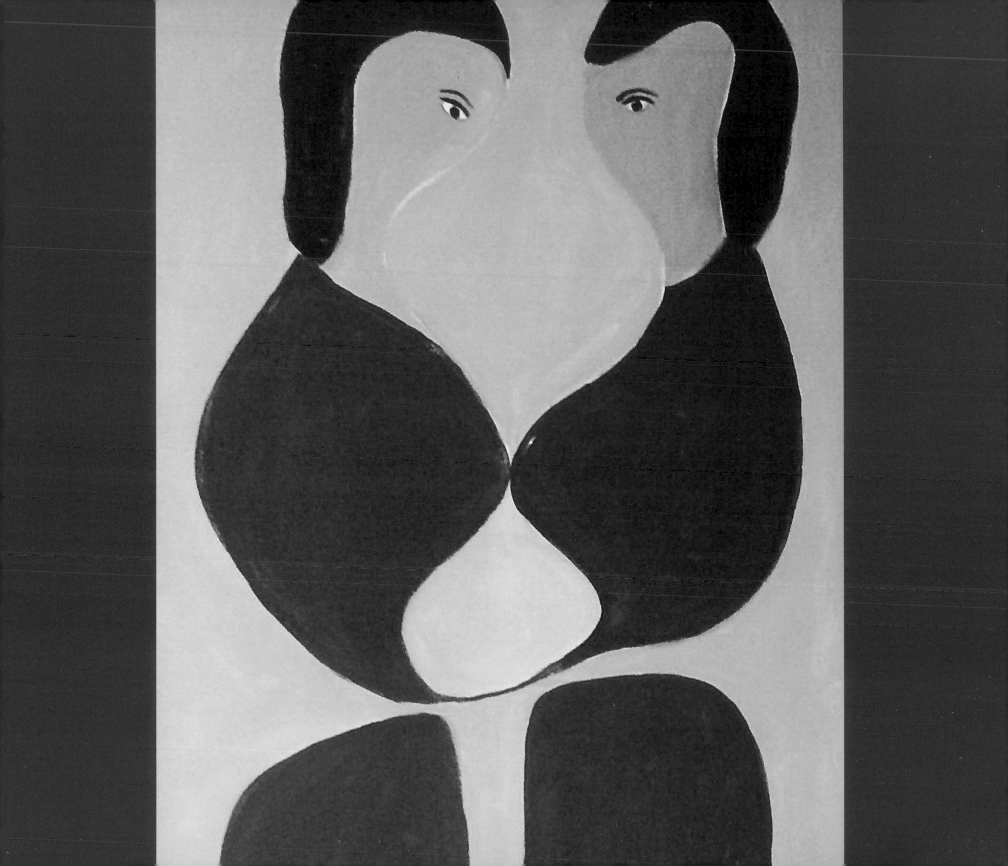

No worry before its time

SHELL GAME, acrylic on canvas, 24" x 28"

Only if we blame, is there reason to forgive

CONVERSATION, acrylic on canvas, 24" x 28"

Solitaire is a state of mind

SOLITAIRE, acrylic on canvas, 30" x 40"

We can either be imperfectly mindful
or perfectly mindless

Rules are made by rulers

STANDING ROOM, acrylic on canvas, 30" x 40"

Don't see it as positive or negative
just see it

Be responsive not reactive

BAR NONE, acrylic on wood, 14" x 17"

It's hard to be soft

TORN, acrylic on canvas, 11"x 17"

To feel expansive, risk being wrong

SELF PORTRAIT, acrylic on canvas, 24" x 28"

Think without the box

JOHN DOWD'S HOUSE, acrylic on wood, 20" x 24"

Passivity robs us of ourselves

HOME RUN, acrylic on canvas, 8" x 9.5"

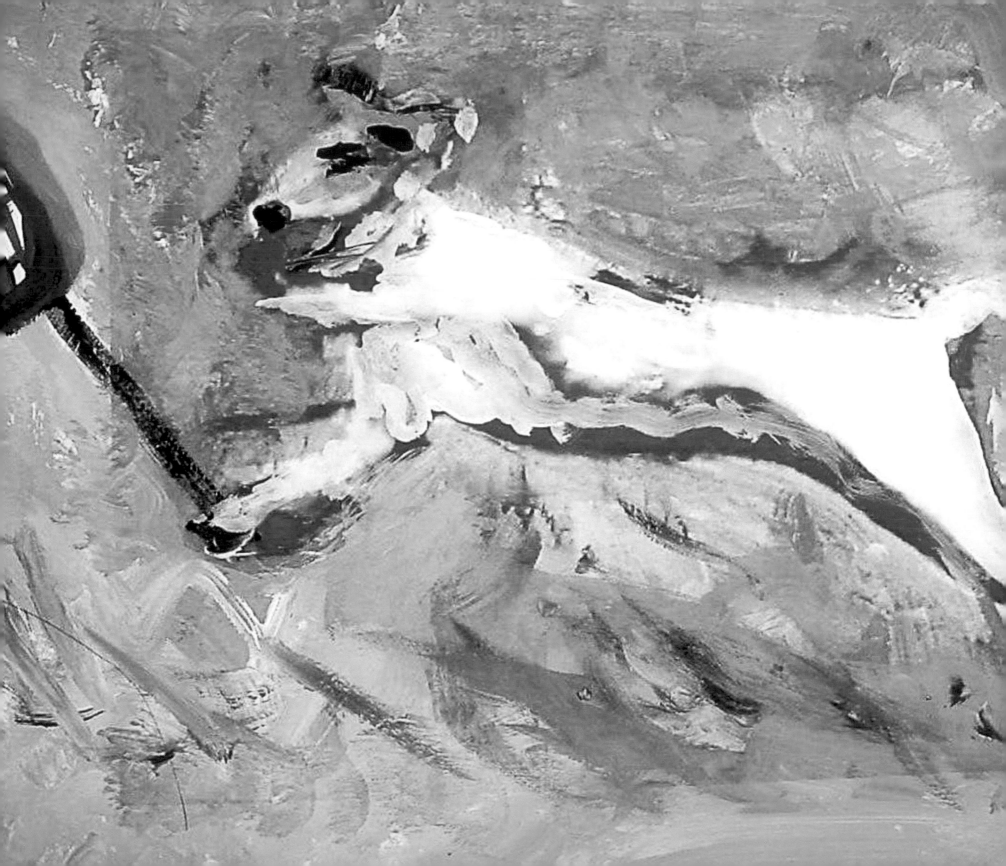

Fight fire with water

Evaluative comparisons are mindless

BOTTOMS UP, acrylic on canvas, 48" x 60"

If you like yourself, it's easier to be yourself

MIRROR MIRROR, acrylic on canvas, 16" x 24"

Mastering is more fun than
having mastered

I THINK I CAN, I THINK I CAN, acrylic on canvas, 8" x 10"

Instead of why, ask why not

FRONT SEAT DRIVER, acrylic on canvas, 7" x 9"

Lazy is just insufficiently motivated

DOG DAY AFTERNOON, acrylic on canvas, 28" x 36"

Life consists only of moments

A DOG'S VIEW, acrylic on canvas, 48" x 60"

Compromise means everyone loses

YOU TALKING' TO ME ? , acrylic on canvas, 8" x 10"

Ask questions, question answers

WOMEN IN WAITING , acrylic on canvas, 36" x 60"

Don't worry about making the right decision, make the decision right

Without doubt, there can be no choice

Embrace uncertainty

INFORMAVORE, acrylic on canvas, 24' 'x 48"

My recipe for a mindful life :
be Generous, Loving, Authentic, Direct, Open
G.L.A.D.O